Boonies

CARL GREEN

PAGE PUBLISHING
Conneaut Lake, PA

First originally published by Page Publishing 2024

ISBN 979-8-89315-836-6 (pbk)
ISBN 979-8-89315-848-9 (digital)

Printed in the United States of America

The Greeter

I walked down the wide bus terminal hallway on a steaming-hot Chicago evening carrying my small military service bag. My new lightweight uniform itched everywhere as I walked. It was new and very nice, but the itching was painful. Some of the people I passed looked at me and smiled, some frowned. It seemed like the hallway went on forever. I had to find the Trailways bus booth, and this dim lighting didn't help. I made my first wrong turn and found the Greyhound terminal! Well, blast, where is the Trailways terminal? Finally, the next right turn put me in sight of it. Hooray!

All this walking and pondering was wearing me out. I needed a place to sit down for a second. The bathroom was across the hall from the Trailways terminal, and in I went. I fished a dime out of my pocket and stuffed it in the toilet slot. All right, I'm finally in! What a ridiculous system to use! I sat down on my favorite chair and took out my half-pint bottle of I. W. Harper and slugged down a shot! What a relief! Nothing like a little help from old I. W. Harper to drive away the bus blues, a real comfort in a time of need! I kicked out my feet and laid back against the toilet tank and relaxed.

After resting for ten long minutes, I concluded it was time to check in with the bus people. On the west-wing hallway, I located the Trailways ticket counter. I walked over and asked the ticket lady for confirmation on my seat to Moline. The nice lady said I was good to go! Super! I'll find a chair and flop. Over by the wall was a bench. It was my lucky day! I sat down there on the bench and scrunched around till I got comfortable—too bad I couldn't take off my boots.

That would definitely bring some relief. I took out my Marlboros and fired up one with my Zippo lighter.

About this time, old I. W. Harper started talking nap time, so I put out the cigarette and slouched back. My eyes just naturally shut, and I started dozing off. Everything was going just fine when out of the blue, this kid grabbed my pocket and asked if he could have one of the medals there. "Well, of course," I said and took one off my uniform to give to him.

Bam! Right out of nowhere, a hand flew over and grabbed my wrist and woke me right up then! I turned to the left and looked at this real old fella right in the eye.

"Say," he said, "you need to save them medals for your family."

Right then, the kid's mother found him and came running over to apologize. "He just loves army stuff," she said. "He has lots of toy soldiers and stuff. He just plays all day with his army guys." She had a good hold on the boy, trying to keep him off me and my medals. Prayers were answered!

"No problem, ma'am," I said. "He seems like a great kid."

The old man looked at me for a minute, and then with a shake of his head, he said, "I was in the cavalry too, but it was a long time ago."

"No fooling?" I said. "Where were you stationed at?"

Well, he looked me hard in the eye. "I served with the first volunteer cavalry," he said.

"That's the one I served with," I said.

"Teddy Roosevelt was our leader," he said. "He led us up to San Jaun Hill, and then he got us going right up the hill, straight into the Cubans' guns!"

"Man, Pops, that's a heck of a story," I said. "What kind of rifle did you use?"

"I had a .30-caliber Krag rifle," he said. "It was a great rifle, but those Cubans had Mauser rifles. They were real good rifles."

"Did the Krags hold tight at two hundred yards?" I asked.

"Oh, heck yeah, they could hit a squirrel easy at that range, with no real kick to worry about either," he said.

"Wish I could get one of those .30 cals," I said. "I could do some nice shooting with it."

"Well, I know I did," he said. "It sure showed what practice can do for a shooter. You know, we never really had a shoulder patch like that big horse one you have. It sure is impressive."

"I guess it gets your attention all right," I said. "The only thing I can tell you is that I will be glad to get home and relax."

"Where are you heading?" he asked.

"I'm going to Bettendorf, Iowa, where my folks live," I told him. "They've been waiting night and day for me to get home, so hopefully I'll make it by tonight."

"I think you will. It can't be more than a couple of hundred miles there, is it?" he asked. "Although if you keep talkin' with I. W. Harper, you might wind up somewhere off the beaten track! Maybe Cuba!"

"You know, I think maybe you are right," I said. "I'll put it away. Say, by the way, what year was that you went up the San Jaun Hill?"

"I believe it was around 1899 sometime," he said. "I can tell you it was hotter than the hinges of hell there!"

"Well, it was really hot in Vietnam," I said. "The temperatures hit the hundreds constantly. All kinds of weather changes along with the high temps. All this and major activity too."

"It must be the same as Cuba," he said. "The jungle temperatures were really high, a lot of malaria too. Our horses were never there with us. Can't say the reason for that, especially for us cavalry guys. We liked to stay glued to those horses."

"Well," I said, "with the time you gave me and the year now, 1968, I figure that you are close to eighty-six years old. Tell me that ain't so?"

"Well, I think you are pretty close to the truth there," he said. "I would never have thought I would live this long. I must have eaten good and did plenty of exercise. Even though I had hope to pass on the exercise."

Right at this time, the PA announced the boarding of his bus. We both stood up and looked over to the waiting line. It wasn't too bad. So Pop grabbed his little suitcase and stood up again. It sounded like he had popped and cracked every joint when he got up! He looked over to the boarding line.

"Well, young fella, I am getting on the bus now. So take care, and have a good trip home," he said.

"Thanks, Pop, you do the same," I said. "Thanks for the pep talk."

*****

Well, today, I think back at that moment in time, and it occurs to me that, that was one heck of a greeting, a real trip back in time with a real hero! He was something else, a major greeter!

A Girl Scout's Christmas

Bong Son, South Vietnam
Christmas Eve 1967

I stood by the sandbags and read the letter again and again. The bag's strings were loose and hanging down. I had opened it and taken out a letter. The bag was a gift from a girl scout troop back home. I found a small steel mirror in there. I felt something else in there, and I turned the bag upside down and shook it. Wow! Two pieces of hard candy fell out in my hand!

The letter said, "Best wishes, soldier, and Merry Christmas." I unwrapped a piece of candy and popped it in my mouth. Great taste! What nice kids! I knew their Christmas would be super. What parents they must have! Real salt of the earth!

I went over to where the cooks were serving chow. They brought stuff out to the LZ (landing zone) in big metal containers. These were insulated for hot and cold. I got in the usual line for chow. I picked up a paper plate and plastic spoon and fork. At least twenty guys were ahead of me, and many were getting in line behind me now. Most of us smoked and told each other about the Green Bags.

A lot of us got one, but only a few received one from the Girl Scouts.

It was beginning to cool off, and the best time of the day was at hand. I took my plate full of Christmas food and went over to sit with my friend John.

"I see you got a Green Bag too, Carl," John said.

"Boy, did I ever," I said. "Mine is from a Girl Scout troop. It's cool."

"I ate my candy already," John said. "I try to always eat my dessert first."

"Yeah, if you get peaches or fruit cocktail in your rats," I said.

Rations came in cans with a special opener nicknamed John Wayne. I guess it's a joke regarding edged weapons or something. For rations (rats), you got a little variety, but the fruit was best, and the ham and limas were the absolute worst! So this Christmas meal was our real treasure! It was so much better with the little Green Bag from the Girl Scouts.

"Where were you today?" John asked.

"We were over in the lost valley," I said, "about four clicks west."

"Thats a long hike," John said.

"It sure is," I said, "and I've got some sore feet to prove it!"

"Then you had a good week," John said. "Nothing but footwork."

"Yeah, right," I said. "Just walking here was one long hot deal."

"Oh, quit gripping," John said. "The army loves you, and you know it."

"No way," I said. "They'd give me some new boots and an R&R if they liked me that much!"

"My Christmas card in the bag," John said, "was sent by a woman. She said Merry Christmas and told me how she was preparing a turkey for their dinner! Wow! I think I might have trouble eating all this!"

"I could eat that," I said. "I remember our dinners. Man, we had gobs of food! There was always this huge bowl piled high with so much mashed potatoes in it! Tons of olives and lots of pumpkin pie! Well, you won't believe it," I said. "Read mine, and let me know what you think."

"Well, I'll be," John said. "Those little Girl Scouts really put it together great!"

"You know, John," I said, "you and I have passed a lot of good days talking and thinking about our futures. This little card tickles me good! Shows even kids can care."

"I wonder what," John said, "this lady was trying to say that wrote me. Was she tired and lonely too or what?"

"Who knows, John?" I said. "Let's go grab some more of that food before all of those other guys eat it all!"

"Yeah," John said. He stood up with his paper plate and tools in one hand and offered to help me up with the other.

"Thanks," I said. "But I'm getting some energy now, and I should be able to get up on my own!"

Well, needless to say, the line was still long, but it was pleasurable standing and talking and comparing past Christmas dinners and all the good stuff at home.

John and I filled our plates again, compliments of General Westmoreland and the US army. We went back to our old seats on our sandbags behind our good bunker. I sat down with my plate of food on my lap and leaned back on the sandbags.

"Wow, John." I breathed out. "I think I might have trouble eating all of this fantastic chow!"

"Why?" John said. "You never had any trouble before."

"Must be I'm wore out," I said, "too much too quick for me."

"Well, just hold up a while," John said. "Just sit back and look at the awesome sunset."

"Yeah," I said, "I wonder if those Girl Scouts are seeing a sunset too? Must be cold there. After all, it is December."

"Yeah," he said. "What a Christmas!"

"I remember when," I said, "I would try to hold it together for days ahead of Christmas, but I just had to ask Mom or Grandma for anything I could dream up! I remember getting a BB gun once. Was I on top of the world over that!"

"Well," John said, "I remember getting cars and clothes and then having a monster ham dinner, with all kinds of fabulous food to eat. Oh my, the pies and cakes, all I could eat!"

"Well, guess what?" I said. "I think we might be close to your house 'cause I'm stuffed full!"

"Ha-ha." John laughed. "I think I am too! I'm just gonna sit here and not move for days!"

There we sat, nibbling away at our super Christmas dinner and dreaming of things at home. The sunset was losing its color now, and darkness was coming in quick. We finally got up and took our paper plates and utensils over to a trash can and had the honor of dumping them in.

"Good night, John," I said.

"Yeah, good night, Carl," John said. "I'll see you tomorrow."

"Maybe for breakfast, huh?" I said.

Of course, breakfast would probably consist of C-rats and instant coffee again! What else is new?

The End

Two Beers

The ground was dry and dusty here in Bong Son, South Vietnam. It was a warm, ninety-degree afternoon. Some rain had fallen yesterday, but the big stuff was still aways away yet. Maybe a month or so still, and then of course, it would be acres and acres of mud. Here in the Central Highlands of South Vietnam, you could expect some hellacious conditions anytime!

It should be a great evening for the camp's movie tonight. It's a new one, and all the people who were lucky enough to have already seen it said it was really great! Man, I just couldn't wait!

I got up off my favorite sandbag chair and slung my rifle over my tired left shoulder where it could bang around all it wanted. We were never allowed to be without a rifle ready to use. I headed over to get some chow at the mess tent. I could smell the food the closer I got to the eternal line, and it was smelling pretty good. The platoon sergeant had set it up so you could get a couple of beers while you walked through the chow line. This way a guy would not get left out and miss his beers—nice of the sarge. Chow started on this little LZ (landing zone) about 5:00 p.m. All of the food was flown in on choppers as usual. They send it out packed in large metal containers to keep it nice and hot. Mostly it was a hundred percent better than a C-ration dinner. You got mashed potatoes, vegetables, and some kind of meat, all of that along with lots of fresh bread and some fruit. Every bite was good eating!

All through the chow line, I had been constantly patting the cargo pockets on my pants and checking on my two beers. They were right where they were supposed to be. I was nervous in the service, I guess. So far, they had not moved to another pocket yet. About this time, five fifteen or thereabouts, I imagined it was starting to get a little bit darker out. So off I went to hunt up my friend John. I wanted to get us a good place to sit and watch the movie.

I found him over in a repair tent playing poker with the dog-handler guys—not too smart. He really should have known better. Those dogs were smarter than all the players by far! John had already lost a couple of packs of cigarettes. He knew the dogs were helping the handlers, but he couldn't see how they were doing it. I could see that it would be necessary for me to render assistance now, or there would be no cigarettes for later.

"Gee, John," I said. "You'd think you would know better than to play with these sharks and their dogs!"

"Oh, I know," John said. "Someday I'm gonna see how they do it."

"Yeah," I said, "right! They will just come clean for you, and then you can head for Las Vegas!"

"Of course," he said. "Hey, what time is it anyway?"

"Almost movie time," I said.

"Well, hold on a few," John said. "I'd like to lose some more."

Both of the dogs were giving me dirty looks now. I sensed the threat and shifted toward the tent's opening—like it would help with a dog the size of Lily! She could move faster than a bullet. Junior, the larger of the two, was an easygoing shepherd. He was slim and liked everyone, me included I hoped!

I watched them skin John for a while. Finally, I got John's attention during the card shuffle and told him we needed to find a good spot fast or we would be sitting too far away to be of any good. John got up and moved away from the table. We said farewell and left the guys to take care of their dogs. There was way too much hair in that tent! You were either rubbing or scratching like one of the dogs constantly, or if all else failed, you could brush hair off everything you owned, including you—a real dog's life!

It really was getting darker now. So we jogged faster over to the bowled-out area of ground where they were preparing to get the movie underway. We found the area I had scouted out before. There were lots of room left. We flopped down and sat for a minute resting. I figured it was dark enough to show the movie now, so what was the holdup?

For the meantime, I sat there. The dirt was just more on my clothes—not to worry, can't have enough dirt! These jungle pants were frayed and had so many holes everywhere anyway, perfectly comfortable and plenty airy. I put my helmet on the ground upside down for a pillow. I tried to make it as comfortable as possible. Not gonna happen. Finally, I just gave up and turned it around back upright so I could get my head in it at an angle. This seemed to work. Super! Okay, now, I've got a pillow. Now for my beer!

There were lots of loud talk and wild comments going around now. Most of the bad ones were going toward the camera guy. He was trying to get the projector going. Get a move on, fella! It looked like he had the reel of a 16 mm film on the sprockets and was ready to go as soon as he thought it was dark enough—for him anyhow. He sure was taking his sweet time setting up.

My head was pillowed on the inside of my helmet. I was still fidgeting around for a more comfortable position. The movie was starting now! At last! The moment was here! I held my church key (beer can opener) up, and just as the show started, I popped the beer can open! What a moment! A profound pleasure!

Then the movie came on: *The Blue Max. What is a Blue Max anyway? Could it be a toilet plunger after it hits the blue water?* The movie was underway now. I kept my eyes on the movie screen, not daring to miss even a single second of the action. Then I licked some of the salt off the beer can and took a sip of the delicious beer! *Oh, I am in heaven now!* Of course, it would end after the two beers, but until then, yeah, only two beers! The army must be afraid of turning us into alkies, typical no-brainers!

The movie started out with trench warfare scenes from the First World War. There was mud everywhere, with soldiers trying to move in it. All of a sudden, some old biplanes flew in and shot at everything—what a horrible mess. It looked just like this little LZ—dirt, trenches, and fortified bunkers all around.

My side ached from lying on it too long, so I rolled over and propped myself up on an elbow. Almost out of salt! Oh, heck, I don't need it; too bad, it was nice to have it with beer though. George Peppard was trying out his plane in the movie now. It seemed he didn't like Wilie, his aristocratic boss. George just went on right by him and got into his old plane and flew off. *That's the right attitude, boy! More beer please.* It was time to open my second one. Oh, what a pleasure! If only I was a millionaire! I would do this forever and ever!

"Carl!" John yelled. "Look at that guy in the black plane."

"What?" I asked. "He's shooting the living heck out of somebody."

"Wow," John said, "I think he just waxed him too."

"Maybe," I said. "It looks like he's going round and round and headed straight downward but awful slow."

Well, the plane landed really hard and bounced around a lot till it stopped. The pilot climbed out of the wreck and seemed to be okay. At least he was walking around, and that was always a good sign. Then out of the clear blue sky came one of the enemy planes and started to shoot at the pilot of the downed plane! What a coward! This bad guy was really a bad character! Who would shoot the guy who had just been shot down and had no way to fight now? He would, I guess. The excitement got to be too much. The whole mob of us were yelling and screaming at the pilot to run! Suddenly, a beer can flew out of the audience and hit smack-dab in the middle of the screen! The beer ran all over the middle of the big bed sheet! It was almost impossible to see the movie now!

Then there were gunshots! One of the guys was shooting his pistol into the movie screen! He was yelling his head off. What was he thinking anyway? The poor screen was soaked with beer now, and the airplanes were really distorted-looking, we couldn't figure out who was shooting at who!

The first sergeant stood up and yelled with his arms flapping away, "Stop the movie! Turn off that blasted projector now!"

By then of course Private Marks had shut down the projector. Now, the uproar was really bad! *What? No movie?* Threats of beatings and other violent acts against the guilty parties were being loudly made! I would have just liked to have smacked those two upside of the head a few times and maybe have taken their beer too! Evidently, it appeared somebody did just that! A few more of the more-able bodies got them pulled apart before we had a full-blown riot going on. Movie time however was definitely over now. Just figures! We were just halfway through the show, and then "that's all, folks."

Well, on the way back to the tent, John was really steamed up. "Oh, this is really bad," John said. "Now we will never know what happened in the movie."

"Oh, well," I said, "maybe we will get to see it again."

"No," he said, "we leave in the morning according to the dog handlers. Who cares anyway? It will just be more hiking and humping the hills. At least we had the day off."

"Well," I said, "you have that exactly right, although those two beers and the hot chow were really very good."

Ears and Ears

The trail went through the bushes and disappeared thirty yards ahead. We had been following this trail for at least a half hour now, and it seemed to be leading us right alongside a small grove of trees. The trees were spread out about thirty feet from each other, and they gave off some nice shade.

This part of the Central Highlands in South Vietnam was just beautiful that morning. The sky was clear, and the temperature had yet to climb up there into the hundred-degree area. As our small perimeter patrol walked along, I kept humming the words to the new song that was out:

> 'Twas the third of June and Billy Joe McCallister
> jumped off the Tallahatchee bridge.

I couldn't stop thinking about this song. It was perpetually recycling though my head, over and over again and again! Sickening! *I must be flipping out. Oh, well, I wonder how the Tallahatchie Bridge compares to the Bong Son Bridge west of here? Probably built by the same people! Whoops! Better watch where I'm putting my boots.* That was not the way to trip and fall. Vines crossed over from one bush to another, and that always caused problems. You either stepped carefully over them or right on top of them. With the old boots I had on, I liked to step on the vines and make a nice soft, quiet cautioned step. The jungle boots wore out awfully fast out here on the trail.

The trail led over between two trees, as I slowly walked along about twenty feet behind John. He was our point man this morning. He always proceeded with extreme care. Many times, the Viet Cong set up trip wires to get you in big trouble. So with my eyeballs bugging out, I moved along with great care. We patrolled this area vigorously because the Viet Cong would love to regain this beautiful valley again. So many rice farms to tax! That would sure help their war effort out a lot. No, thanks! The Viet Cong had been beaten badly this year and were not out in force in the valleys like they were accustomed to doing. Often we got to see some of their violent atrocities perpetrated upon their countryman—not pretty at all.

Stumbling along, I was a little lax on my attention when John hissed out loud to me. *What the hay? What's up now?* I cautiously moved up to where he was kneeling down and looking out through the bushes. *What is this? It looks like a small farm! I mean, it looks like one from Iowa! There's corn planted there! That can't be. After all, this is Southeast Asia, not the Midwest USA. There is supposed to be rice here, not corn! This bears inspection by golly!*

Off John and I went, carefully stepping through the cornstalks. They had reached a height of about four feet, and the tassels were hanging out on top of the plants. Hard to believe! Corn in South Vietnam! What's next? Our whole seven-man patrol stood and stared at the corn in the field. We couldn't believe our eyes.

"What do you think, John?" I asked. "Is it ripe or not?"

"How would I know?" he said. "You're from that area, aren't you?"

"Well, sort of," I said. "Illinois and Iowa are next to each other and raise a lot of corn there."

"What do you think?" John said. "Will Poppa San blow fuse if we hog some of his precious corn?"

"I don't think I'd do that," I warned him. "He might get awfully upset about some GI ripping off his corncobs."

The corn row suddenly parted, and out came two young Vietnamese boys, with big grins on their faces. I just knew they had been hiding back in the corn row, listening to us idiots admiring their corn patch! I still had my little gray Brownie camera in my pocket. What a great opportunity! I approached the boys and fumbled around a bit, attempting to converse with them in my very limited Vietnamese. They stood there in front of their corn patch while I took their picture. I thanked them—nice kids and a nice place.

I went over and moved an ear around a bit. It looked like it was getting close to being ready to eat. The stalks looked solid and were good and green. Always a good sign, I had learned. Maybe the Vietnamese would dissolve these stinking rice paddies. Who knows? I decided to hit the road and look around this place. We walked around the end row of corn, and lo and behold, there stood a house! It was up on stilts to keep it out of the water and monsoon mud. The house had a veranda-style porch across the side. It looked cool and comfortable with lots of places to sit and yak at each other—nice.

While John and I were staring at the house, Pappa San came out the doorway and stood on the porch. He started waving at us to come on up and talk, and he acted very friendly. *Why not?* I thought, *Maybe this is a good time to show some of that "hearts and minds" stuff that the big shots are harping on all of the time. Might get some corn out of this deal too!*

While the other guys stayed out in the front yard, John and I walked over to Pappa San. He smiled and clapped his hands together several times. I had learned early on that this was usually a good sign and that it was a fairly safe place, not to worry.

Pappa San started pointing out things around his yard: the small well and some chickens running around really happy. You could almost picture yourself on a Groucho Marx farm! It sure had a long, long way to go to be an Iowa farm, but he was giving it his all, so good for him! His attitude seemed to change when we went over to look at his corn again. I held my hand on the top tassel and then raised my hand up high above the cornstalk. He caught on right away that the corn could get a lot taller—another smart farmer. Of course, one look at his corn, and you knew he didn't even come close to believing me. Oh, well, I tried. Pappa San pointed up at the house. It dawned on me that we should go up and grab a chair. I was all for this. My feet were sore and really would like a break.

Ed and Bill had squatted down on the back corner of the porch in the shade and were shooting the breeze with the two boys. It must be good 'cause the boys were hopping around all over the porch! Of course, those guys were known for some tall tales. It was an exciting time for the boys as they were talking to real army guys. It looked like Ed had shared a hard candy bar with them to boot! Their cheeks were puffed out and jaws a-chomping away.

My chair was pretty worn-out, so I decided to just sit on the floor with my back against the wall. It was nice and shady and comfortable. Pappa San was pointing at the sky and then pointing down. It looked like he was wondering if it would rain or not. Maybe he was hoping for snow. That would really make the *Stars and Stripes* headlines! *Oh, man, this is so nice to sit here and flop. I think my feet have had enough and decided to just retire!*

After about a half hour, I pointed around the farm at different things. Then I pointed at the corn and mimed eating an ear! Old Pappa San looked at me and held my eye for a minute and then just shook his head. No way! This was his pride and joy. I tried again but got the same answer. So that idea went out the window.

I got up and took a minute to stretch the kinks out. I politely bowed to Pappa San. I grinned at him and thanked him for the nice visit. Then down the steps John and I went with some friendly waves to the kids and Pappa San, and we all started moving out into the trees again. The two boys came right along with us! Ed stopped them and started his Groucho act by pointing back at the house and shooing them along. They reluctantly started back to the farm disappointed that they couldn't be army men, I guess. They still gave us some great big cheers and waves! It was a wonderful farm, a mini Iowa palace, minus the crows!

Bat Soup

I picked up a cardboard box of C-rations and looked at the label. It was beans and something. It had sat on the 105 mm empty wooden cartridge storage box I was using for my only furniture. It worked great! I just sat there in the mud and stayed filthy dirty. The other two ration boxes were incomplete. A full new box would have a can of fruit, some type of meat, miniboxes of cigarettes, toilet paper, maybe some type of cake, and some peanut butter and crackers. The only silverware was the John Wayne can opener. I think it got this name because you had to be tough to get it to open the cans of food. It would just about kill your fingers to hold it and keep on turning and cutting the lid off your rations.

The two incomplete boxes only had a can of ham and lima beans and a can of peaches. All the other empty cans I had set on the ammo box for decoration. These were my only real food connection to homecooked meals! Next to the boxes, I had a small pile of salt and pepper packets. I just liked to save them—a real pack rat, even got the mud to prove it!

The monsoons were here, which meant the rain never stopped day or night. Living in the bunkers underground was a muddy experience, mud on everything around and under. There was also a sea of mud outside of the bunker. "Some home away from home" was what I referred to it. The mud squeezed into my boots and stuck there forever it seemed, mud and more mud, mud for everything from food to hair to stuff. When I would wake up in the morning, I'd have mud dried solid in my socks, mud-packed toes, and curly toenails!

Division supply brought water and rations out here to the LZ (landing zone) for us boonie rats to use. Water was stored outside with the mud in a big canvas bag. It was hung up on a wooden frame so you could hold your canteen under a spigot and fill it up. My folks had sent me a care package with a lot of presweetened Kool-Aid in it. This was my favorite drink at this fabulous resort.

About five thirty, at this time of day, the sun would get ready to go down. The rain still kept on coming down, fast and slow, on and on. It was getting dark out, and everything there stopped completely then, not much movement. No lighting was allowed outside of blacked-out bunkers. It was cold and wet, with plenty of mud, just plain miserable weather.

Inside our little two-man bunker, John and I sat on our worn-out canvas army cots and talked about all the different kinds of meals to be had, anything from enchiladas to bacon and eggs. Fried catfish was discussed at some length. Potato salad was my best topic. I would close my eyes and think of the "potatey" egg taste. Pretty soon, John yelled at me for drooling in the mud like an idiot.

Oh, for some of Grandma's potato salad! I remembered all those big picnics we had with such great food. Grandma would be in the kitchen up to her elbows cooking all those goodies. Sometimes, I wouldn't quite get my fingers out of the way in time, and the spatula would come away the winner!

Well, so much for culinary appetite. I decided to create a new boonie rat special tonight. The can of beans and wieners would get mixed up with whatever was left in the other boxes, and I'd add enough water to soup it up really good, genius at work, a real Einstein at work in the muddiest kitchen in Vietnam!

"Okay, John," I said, "here's the plan. I'm going to mix all this stuff together and heat it up."

"Oh, no," John said, "not another miracle waiting to happen! Can't we just eat the regular slop? I mean what's to be gained from all the extra time? We already know what the junk tastes like from past experience."

"Look here," I said, "I've got this all figured out so that one taste will hide the other. That way you won't be able to taste the ham and beans at all!"

"This is it," John said. "This is why there are monsoons. For people to drive themselves nuts over food!"

"Well," I said, "what else is there to do but starve creatively and sit here and listen to the TV shows on a little transistor radio?"

"I don't know," John said, "but it would sure be super nice to think of something totally different for a change!"

"Well," I said, "what's tonight's TV show going to be?" All of the radio programs were just that, rebroadcast TV programs. "*Gunsmoke, I Love Lucy*, or what? Hanoi Hannah maybe? She broadcast psycho stuff from North Vietnam just to bug us GIs. Oh, well, at least we get to hear how awful we are!"

"Last I heard," John said, "it was going to be *Gunsmoke* first and then *Batman* after that."

"Wow," I said, "a real thrill ride if I ever saw one. That's it then, huh? Just Hanoi Hannah. Is she still on our case or what?"

"There just might," John said, "be a potato chip commercial after Hanoi Hannah shoots her mouth off for a while. 'Sides, I'd like to hear some of her dorky stuff."

"She's ridiculous," I said. "Who could even believe the stuff she says? Dumb and dumber. Man, that potato chip commercial sounds so good, I could just eat them all! Might even be worth staying up late just to hear it."

"Aw, Carl," John said, "don't do that. You'll start drooling all over, and then the rats will come on back!"

Well, anything but that! About a week ago, during the night, I was snoring away, dreaming about my big collie dog and how he would always cuddle up to me at night. About two at dawn, I woke up and felt something move near my leg. At first I just knew it was one of those monster pit vipers that bite into you at night. Now I was shaking bad. I felt it again on my leg, and it was hairy all right! It was a rat about the size of a cat, a real big rat! I flew off the cot and tried to kick it out the doorway. It must have known it was facing a number 11 combat boot and had no chance, so out the door it flew! I sat down and kept right on shaking. John of course provided me with an accurate account of the actual happening for hours and hours.

Therefore, tonight, I would be more careful with my food preparations than usual. We used chemical heat tablets to cook our food. You had to set the tablets on the ground and light them with the ration matches. They burned slowly while you held your mess kit pan over the fire. Then when your hand cramped up really bad, the food should be done one way or another! What an effort for a hill of beans, luxury living!

The little transistor radio squeaked out the thrills of *Gunsmoke*, with all the fun going on at the Long Branch Saloon. Doc and Kitty were arguing about something wrong with one of Doc's patients. Marshall Dillon stomped in and grabbed a chair and smiled his way around the table but stopped when he saw Kitty. Of course, there was nothing wrong with my imagination. I guess that the Long Branch Saloon was famous all over the world.

I mixed up all the special ingredients in the mess kit pan and lit the cooking tablets. Using one hand, I maintained a solid grip on the pan handle and used my other hand to hold on to the spoon to stir up this digestive masterpiece! It actually seemed to smell better. This must be where "hope eternal" comes into play.

Then *Batman* came on now! Evidently, the Joker was doing something bad. Commissioner Gordon was talking to Batman on the bat phone about the rotten Joker! My dinner was almost ready now. My arm ached from holding the pan over the fire that long. It was hard enough to cook this great dish, let alone listen to my favorite show. *Wow! Pow! Bam! Whap!* That was it! I decided to call it my Bat Soup! I just knew I would be inspired about something tonight—Bat Soup with all the *wow and pow* you want to put in it! *Hey, I could even send this recipe to Batman, and he can have his butler, Alfred, cook it up in the great bat cave! Might even give the Dynamic Duo a power boost!* I thought.

I'll have to remember all these ingredients too. Let's see, a package of salt, a can of beans and wieners, and a can of ham and beans. Ugh, makes you sick thinking of it. Oh, and I did crumble some crackers into the mess too. This could be as famous as that jambalaya, maybe as great as Christmas cookies! Oh, wow, pow!

"John," I said, "listen! I've got it. A great new food recipe. I just named it Bat Soup."

"Nuts!" John said. "You've gone batty is what it is. Too much *Gunsmoke* in your *Batman*."

"No," I said, "no, it really has a better taste! You've got to try this. It's great!"

"I don't know," John said. "It looks bad. Can I put salt on it? Maybe the rat would eat it then."

"Please," I said, "don't bring up rats at the dinner table! It just ruins my appetite thinking about the miserable things."

"All right," John said, "dish me up some of that Bat Soup, and I'll try gagging it down."

So up to our ankles in mud, we sat on the worn-out old cots and hunched over our nice hot meal of Bat Soup! It wasn't too bad to start out, but after my tastebuds caught on that it was just the same old, same old rations, it was gag-it-down time again! So went the rest of the evening. After *Batman*, I got to feeling sleepy, so I crashed out on my cot for the evening.

High Heels

I opened the main exit door to the hospital and stepped out into the heat of the morning. It felt to be in an oven after air-conditioning in the hospital, humid and very hot. There was the little hospital shuttle bus sitting there, waiting for all of us repaired able bodies to hop on. I had a flight to the First Cavalry's base camp at An Khê. I got on the shuttle bus and sat in a hot middle seat. It warmed me right up fast! There were only three of us to go, so there was plenty of room but not a lot of shade.

The bus left Quy Nhon Hospital and took us to the compound gate. The bored MP at the gate waved us on through. It was only a short trip to the helicopter landing pad. I hopped off the shuttle and found the ground markers for the First Cav helicopter pad. Some enterprising GI had built a nice chair out of sandbags, so I flopped down on it, only to realize I had just sat down on the hot seat! I wondered how long it would be before I get a ride to An Khê? I was awfully glad to be out of that hospital and heading back to my unit. I had been sent there three days ago with a boil infection on the left side of my head that was hideous and very infected. The doctors worked on it, and the nurses kept it from getting a lot worse. They crammed enough pills in me that nothing could ever make me sick again. I'm glad to be gone and real glad to feel good again.

The sandbags were getting comfortable, and my nice jungle fatigues were stiff but clean feeling. The sweat was soaking them good now out in this heat. I took out my Marlboro smokes and shook one out. There was nothing else to do but sit tight and wait for my helo ride.

"Hong Kong" mountain
An Khê, South Vietnam, 1967
ở đằng kia kìa

Somewhere near a half hour later, a chopper started its approach toward the landing pad I was waiting at. I covered my face as it flared into land. Dirt and dust flew like mad all over my nice new fatigues! Oh, well, it had to happen sooner or later. I could barely see the helicopter crew chief waving me over. I scrunched down and waddled over to the side door. I put a foot on the skid and grabbed the doorframe. With a big heave, I went up and in. I sat down quickly on the web seat and found a safety belt. Safety belts are a thing of necessity in a helicopter mainly because the doors are usually left open for cool air. The pilot must have gotten the crew chief's OK because the engine started cranking over a lot faster and the blades were biting the air good. We were moving forward and up. This was one of the best Hueys, a gunship from the First Cav's 228th aviation, on time all the time!

The air was so much cooler up high in the sky. The wind blew through my wet clothes so nice and cool. I loved it! It was a wonderful day to be up in the sky. It was hot down there but perfect up here.

It was a short twenty-minute ride to the First Cav's base camp at An Khê. As we came down in position over the landing pad, the heat had increased. We went from seventy with a nice breeze to ninety and a too-hot-to-handle ground temperature! Man was it *hot*!

I got off the helicopter and headed over to report to the transient officer. The officer told me I was being assigned to a forward detachment. I was told to load up anything I had left and wait for a ride. The company first sergeant had sent along all my worldly possessions when I left to go to the hospital. Here they were waiting for me in a small green bag. Jeez, was that all I owned? Man, even a mouse had more than I did! I found an empty cot in the transient barracks and lay down for a nap. It would be many hours before I could leave, maybe after chow time at four thirty.

After my hour nap, I started thinking I should go into town for some boring pastime as there was nothing here to do. I could get some Vietnamese junk and send it home to my brothers and sisters. *Thats it! I'll do it. They might like something exotic. Might even have Vietnamese Barbie dolls! Who knows?* I thought.

I grabbed my hat and headed out of the barracks and went straight to the company HQ tent. Everyone knew I was leaving that afternoon, so I was sent right to the first sergeant, the big boy himself!

"Come on in," the first sergeant yelled.

I patted the dust off my new shirt with a few swats of my hat and went on into his official tent area. I stopped in front of his field desk and asked. "Top," I said, "I'm leaving this beautiful domain today, so is there any way I could go to town this afternoon?"

"Well, I suppose that's possible," he said, "but only for a couple of hours because I don't want you to miss your ride out."

"I can return before three in the afternoon," I told him. "After all, there isn't much to do there either."

"I tell you what," Top said, "you go, but you bring me back some beer."

"Okay," I said, "that's a deal."

Out the tent, I went straight to the motor pool. *What a great day!* I thought. *I am even being allowed to use a jeep today! They must really want me out of here for real.*

"Hey, Mike," I said. "Top gave me permission to use his jeep for a few hours this afternoon."

"Are you nuts?" Mike said. "I have to see some authorization for you to get his personal jeep. Otherwise, no deal."

Main St., An Khê

"Call him on the phone set," I told him. "He'll tell you I'm good to go."

So Mike got on the phone set and secured permission for me to go on and use the first sergeant's jeep—what a bunch of bull.

"Now," Mike said, "I want you to drive carefully."

"Aw, come on." I growled. "I'm probably the top driver in this unit."

"Boy, are you nuts?" Mike said loudly and grinned at me. "How long are you going to take it?"

"Well," I said, "probably only a couple of hours at the most."

"Okay," Mike said as he shoved a couple of papers at me, "sign on these sheets, and adios, amigo."

I hustled over and got in the jeep's worn-out driver's seat. I cranked up the motor and eased it into gear. I drove slowly away from the HQ motor pool area. When I was out of sight of the HQ, I floorboarded the gas pedal and roared off. I headed for the village of An Khê in high gear as fast as the jeep would go!

Out the main perimeter gate at the First Cavalry division base Camp Radcliff I went and down the road into the east end of town. *Whoopee!* The shacks and buildings were really bad. People lived and worked here as best they can though. I got to hand it to them.

Because of the war, all money was regulated. I had some piastre and some script moolah. *Let's see what I can find to send home*, I thought. I pulled off the main highway and parked in front of a store with its awning shading all kinds of merchandise. There were lots of odds and ends here. *Well, let's see. Girls like dolls and stuff. Maybe this will work after all.* I picked up a plastic doll about fifteen inches tall and gave it to Mama San to set up on the counter. As soon as I set it down, the flies swarmed back all over it and the counter. Gee! I kept hunting around the shop, smashing flies and talking to myself.

I was getting tired and felt like taking a couple of aspirin as a reward for having to listen to Mama San blab for an hour nonstop! I didn't even understand what she was saying. She was probably reciting the Pledge of Allegiance over and over again!

Oh, boy, look at that, I thought. There it was, the perfect gift—a beautiful emerald-green Oriental embroidered dress, just perfect for my sister Sue! *Wait, those little painted high-heeled shoes would really look great with that dress.* I decided to take them too. Okay, I finally had what I needed. It was time to figure out how much Mama San wanted to shut up!

"Okay, Mama San," I said loud enough for her to hear me over her continued racket, "how much?"

"Ohh, bookoo piastra, GI," she said. "Khong bao nhieu, Nam dong thoi" (Not much, only five dong).

"Okay," I told her and nodded my head. "Take what you want."

"Duoc roi," Mama San told me (meaning "Okay"). She reached out and took some of the cash I was holding up. It looked about right.

I put the doll and shoes in one bag and the dress in another and headed out to the jeep. It was still there smiling at me just waiting to go—what a nice little jeep. I started it up and drove slowly back to the main gate at the base camp. After passing through the main gate, I drove over to the supply area. I found the right place for beer and cigarettes. It was so far down the alley of tents that you wanted to give up before you even started. But I had promised Top that I would grab some beer for him on the way back from town. I pulled over by the supply tent and shut off the jeep. I just sat there and relaxed. After all, I was on my time today. After about five minutes, I left the jeep and went into the supply tent.

"What's up?" the supply sergeant said.

"I'm here to get some beer," I said. "It's for the first sergeant's mess at our company."

"Oh, yeah," the buck sergeant said. "He called and said he was sending you over for a load of beer."

"How about a couple of cases for me too?" I said.

"Ha-ha. That's a laugh," he said. "I can hardly steal any for myself, let alone you guys."

"Well," I growled, "load up Top's beer. I'm in a hurry to get to the post office and mail out some presents home."

He loaded three cases of beer into the back of the jeep and then had me sign on the dotted line for them—must really want the Top to get his beer.

I finally made it to the post office area and went and asked the GI postal clerk how to send the gifts for my sisters back home. He gave me a decent-size box that held everything. I packed it all into the box and put a note on top of the clothes before sealing it up. After I addressed the stuff, he set it on the outgoing table and said that was it.

I left the postal tent and headed back to the company and the first sergeant's tent with his beer. *Hopefully, he would let me have a six-pack. Very doubtful, but there's always hope,* I thought.

*****

Many, many years later, about forty-five, if I remember right, I got a phone call from my nephew Joe.

"Hey, Uncle," he said. "I've got some of your stuff here at my mom's house. What do you want to do with it?"

"Hold on now," I told him. "I don't have anything there. What the heck are you talking about?"

"Maybe you should come over and check it out," Joe said.

"Okay," I told him. "I can come over this afternoon somewhere around two thirty."

"That's great," Joe said, "because I don't know what to do with it."

I finally arrived at my sister Sue's old house about two or so and found both of my nephews, Joe and John, boxing up and doing a general cleanup around the place. My sister had passed away, and they were trying to get the house ready to sell. They took me into my sister's old bedroom, where a lot of old clothes were laid on the bed and stacked in boxes on the floor.

Joe held up a zippered clothing case large enough for a suit to hang inside. He unzipped the case, and lo and behold, there was the dress and painted high-heeled wooden shoes that I had sent home from Vietnam many, many years ago! My sister had kept them cased in her closet all this time without my knowledge! My breath caught in my throat. This was so unbelievable! Amazing! All this time, and she never said a word to me. At that moment, I thought, *What am I going to do with them now? I guess they'll have to hang in my closet till I can figure out something or other to do with them.* Well, guess what, they are still here!

Kool-Aid Kid

The rain continued to slowly but surely wash away my whole stash of Kool-Aid. My worn-out jungle fatigues were now tie-dyed. Different colored streams of Kool-Aid were running down the front of my jungle shirt. Streams of red and blue Kool-Aid were washing right down my forearms. My shirt pockets were swelled out with water and soggy paper packaging coming out of the pockets.

This was so bad! All the Kool-Aid packs from my care package were ruined now. Doom! Now, it will be nothing but bad-tasting water for weeks. All of our drinking water was sent out in lister bags. The choppers usually came here once a day with our dinner and other supplies. If the weather was rotten, it could be a week! For now, we had nothing but cans of rations for eats.

I scraped up some of the Kool-Aid packs from my care package with my hands. What a mess. Such despair! Well, I can at least lick up some of the Kool-Aid. After a few minutes of intense licking, I got a little satisfaction from the loss of my Kool-Aid stash. Bits of odd-colored paper stuck all over my face and arms. My shirt was plastered with bits of paper. I spit out the extras and felt a little better over my loss.

My care packages came from home. My mom and grandma would cram in a couple of Jiffy Pop popcorn tinfoil pans along with socks, pictures, letters, and lots of Kool-Aid packages. They put in photographs of home events and stuff. Sometimes, they didn't know what else to shove in the box, so they threw in lots more Kool-Aid packs for padding. It worked great! I traded the extras for all kinds of goodies.

Well, the little half-submerged foxhole with a tent for a top had fallen in on my partner, John, and me that afternoon. It seemed the early monsoon rain had drenched us a little too much. The foxhole had a least six inches of water in it. Everything we owned was floating around in the water. My partner, John, said, "The heck with it," and went looking for some place dry. I was abandoned. So there I stood in the water with part of my tent all torn. Everything I could hang on to was sopping wet. My clothes of course were soaked. So with all my Kool-Aid soaking into my OD uniform, I was a real GI scarecrow!

The rain had stopped. Well, now was the time for sergeants to pop out of their holes and start with the dufus orders, like "Clean up that hole, Carl." Well, I hoped the monsoon would hold up for the afternoon. That should be enough time for me to salvage the leftover shredded Kool-Aid packs. *Yep, sure enough, here the sarge comes,* I thought.

"Boy, Carl," Sergeant Meyer said. "What happened to you? You look like you were splattered with shredded newspaper!"

"Well," I said. "The tent's top fell on John and me. Then the rain let us have it real good. Everything I own has been damaged."

"Hey," Sergeant Meyer said, "you don't own anything, at least not now. Ha-ha!"

"Thanks a lot," I said. "You sure know how to beat up on a guy, Sarge."

"Oh, Carl," he said, "come on, you know this is the life! Look at you. You look like heck with bits of paper stuck on your nose and even on your ears!"

"That's it," I said. "If you can't appreciate a thing of beauty, then you are no longer my sergeant."

"Oh, ho," he said. "I suppose I've always been your personal handpicked sergeant."

"I wish," I said. "I had picked a nice, fat mess sergeant."

"Aha," Sergeant Meyer said, "does this mean you are ready for KP duty [kitchen police, dishwasher]?"

"Not on your life," I said. "Just because I complain about the monsoon rain. Not to mention my foxhole swimming pool. That doesn't mean I am ready for foreign service to the mess hall!"

"It sounded like it to me," he said. "No one in the whole platoon has your ability to complain. No one even comes close."

"You know," I said, "I learned it right here in Uncle Sam's army. Aren't you the proud teacher, Sarge!"

"Got to go," Sarge said. "I have to go and supervise the rest of the super troopers."

"You do that," I said. "Be very clear with the world's greatest troopers. Above all, don't tell them the truth about anything. Even if it hurts you!"

"Don't worry," Sarge said, "I'll pass the word to all those super troopers to kick in some cash. Then we can get you a nice yellow rubber ducky."

"Sarge," I said, "come back tomorrow when you're all better."

"Take care," he said. "This whole area is a real mess."

Off the sarge went heading toward the officers' tents, probably going to volunteer me for KP—what a superb noncommissioned officer mentality, perfect army material. *How could anyone like the army?* There had to be a midget under a counter somewhere that determined who's who, probably gives the guys a color test. When they identify the color green, they would be in like Flynn!

Man oh man! I've got to get out of this country. This is positively my last and only visit to the beautiful Southeast Asian country of Vietnam. I'm going back to south-central Los Angeles. Maybe I can develop further up the line from abject poverty. I should probably set a goal in life. What? I have no idea, I said to myself in silence.

Then, I was back to bailing the water out of my foxhole. I had been using my steel helmet to scoop out the water. Some of the water had changed to Kool-Aid colors—really nice-looking slop. *What a palace! Just right for the Jolly Green Giant. He would have a wonderful chance to grow another ten feet taller with all this water I'm throwing out,* I thought.

After about an hour of scooping out water and salvaging my good junk, I finally found some fairly solid ground. It was time to fix the tent top and have it ready for the next big rain, which came down heavy in great big drops. It made me glad I've got a steel pot to wear on my head! The canvas shelter top was so bad off that I didn't want to even try putting it up again, but us beggars were not allowed to be choosy. So up it went. I pulled the tent over the tops of the sandbag wall and roped it down. Then I went under the tent and pushed the center support pole up as far as possible. Outside I went and chugged around the tent, pulling and tightening up the tent support guidelines.

I went inside the smelly canvas tent and piled what was left of my good stuff up on my army cot. *Maybe it will dry up in here a little bit,* I thought. There was more monsoon weather on the way. Now that the wet season was here, one could expect the mud to become really deep. I gave the tent-foxhole a quick once-over and decided it would just have to do. It was time to go get some chow.

About the Author

Carl Green graduated high school in 1965. A few months later, he was in the army. He was sent to Vietnam in 1967 after a short stay in Germany. After the military, he wandered around for a while and finally attended junior college for a few semesters. He went to work as a carpenter, which led to a lifetime occupation. He retired from the carpenter union after working in nuclear plants for thirteen years.

www.ingramcontent.com/pod-product-compliance
Lightning Source LLC
Chambersburg PA
CBHW021813150726
47989CB00004B/1914